Spelunking Through Life

David H. Rosen

Robert Epstein
Foreword

art by Diane Katz

Rosenberry
books,
etc.

RESOURCE *Publications* · Eugene, Oregon

Also by David H. Rosen

Patient Centered Medicine: A Human Experience
(with Uyen Hoang)

Time, Love and Licorice: A Healing Coloring Storybook

Clouds and More Clouds

The Tao of Elvis
(a Rosenberry Books/Wipf & Stock edition)

The Healing Spirit of Haiku
(with Joel Weishaus)

Evolution of the Psyche
(with Michael Luebbert)

The Tao of Jung: The Way of Integrity

Transforming Depression:
Healing the Soul Through Creativity

Medicine as a Human Experience
(with David Reiser)

Lesbianism: A Study of Female Homosexuality

ISBN: 978-1-4982-9392-1

Designed by Rosenberry books, etc.
101 Nicks Bend West
Pittsboro, NC 27312
800.723.0336 919.969.2767
www.rosenberrybooks.com
Rosenberry books, etc. is a registered trademark.

Wipf & Stock is an imprint of Wipf and Stock Publishers.
199 W. 8th Ave., Suite 3
Eugene, OR 97401
wipfandstock.com

Foreword

Are you in touch with the basic five senses you were born with?
Do you know how to travel and when to stop?
Can you listen — in darkness — to that still, small voice within?
Then you have all that you need to weather the beginnings and endings of life, which unfolds along the serpentine road of relationship.
Life, after all, is relationship.

So maintains David H. Rosen in the disarmingly simple, beautiful book of haiku in your hands (enriched by the unadorned art of Diane Katz). One need not possess Olympic Gold to embark; it's perfectly okay to trip over the door frame with the first step of this journey. That misstep may even be an auspicious sign, depending on one's perspective: Freudian, Jungian or "other." In the exploration of caves, stumbling can slow one down enough to discover something — or someone — precious.

Don't ever think you are too old to love or to be reborn. Maybe Love itself is the path that fires up the senses: sight, sound, smell, touch, taste, movement and stillness. With enough curiosity, any one of the senses can precipitate transcendence. If you summon the courage to love, you will find your way to the Holy land of aliveness and fulfillment, as this vibrant retired psychiatrist has. That place may be in a foreign land, a local river, a nearby meadow, or your own kitchen window. Did you wake up in a cave? There are blessings to behold in what we might call the unborn, the deathless. Go ahead, take a step, or set a spell.

Robert Epstein , El Cerrito, CA

Outside of a dog,
a book is man's best friend.
Inside a dog, it's too dark to read.

attributed to Groucho Marx

SPELUNKING
Through Life

David H. Rosen, MD

art by Diane Katz

For Willow

(when our rescued dog was dying)

Willow's head on
blue monkey boy…
nearing doggie heaven

First glimpse of the new year—
tripping on the door frame

Blue dragonfly —
what do you
listen to?

River oak swaying…
silence

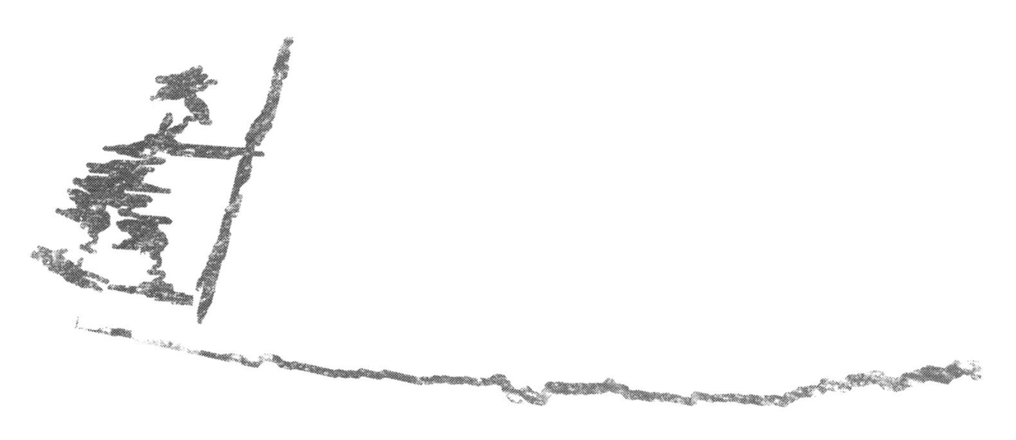

Cinnamon foxglove
pierces
field of dry grass

Divorce...
peeling an onion

In a deep dark cave…
finally light and
a way out

Seeing a Freudian...blue moon,
a Jungian...full moon

Snow-capped
grey clouds...
crack of thunder

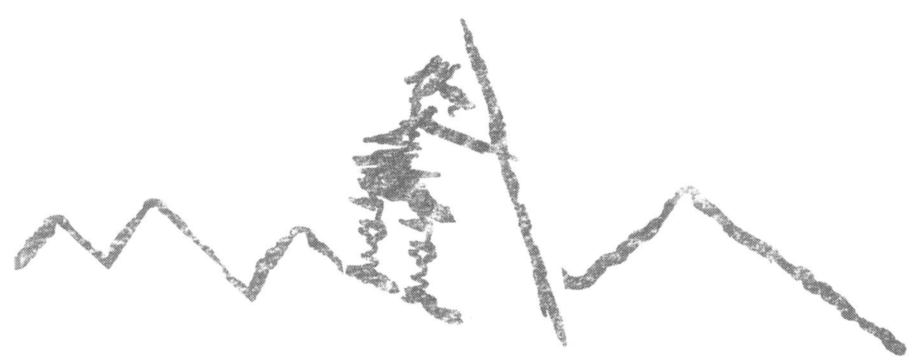

Fiery clouds
over a red barn—
green apples turning

Snake…
dead or alive?

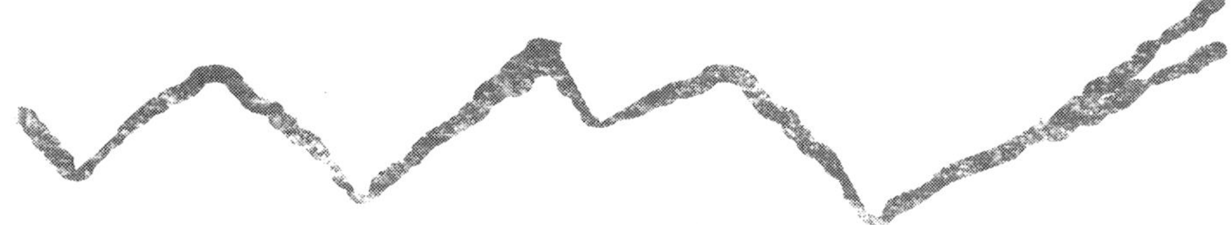

Spelunking through life...

there is a way out

Machu Picchu
face to face
with a llama

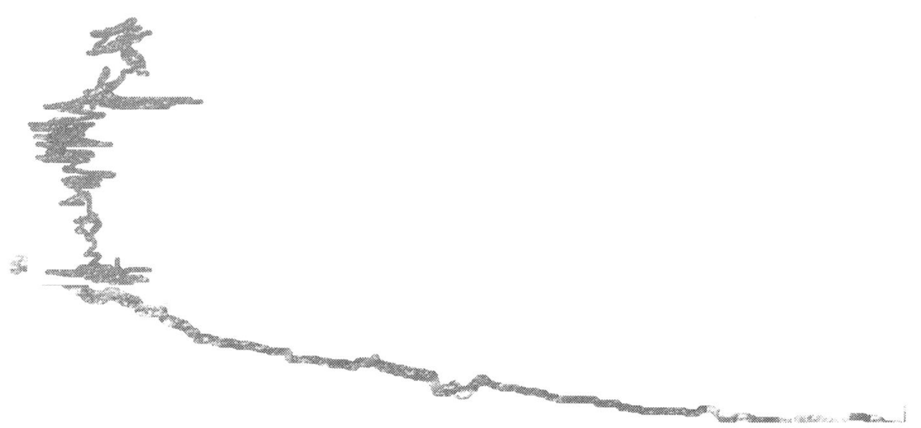

Lost in Kiwiland and
meeting Lanara...
there is a goddess

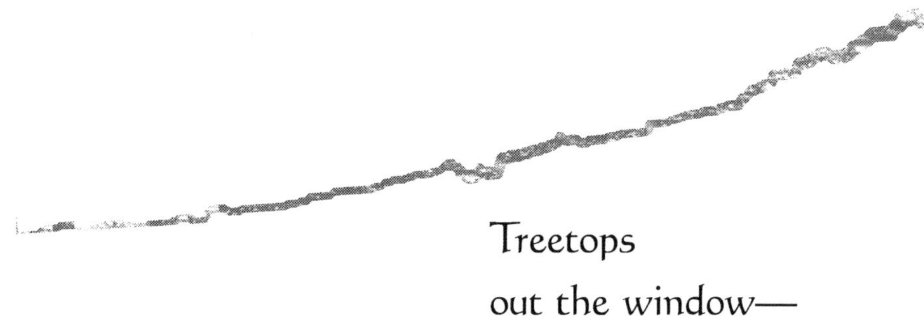

Treetops
out the window—
cooking chorizo

Darkness…
shooting star
haiku

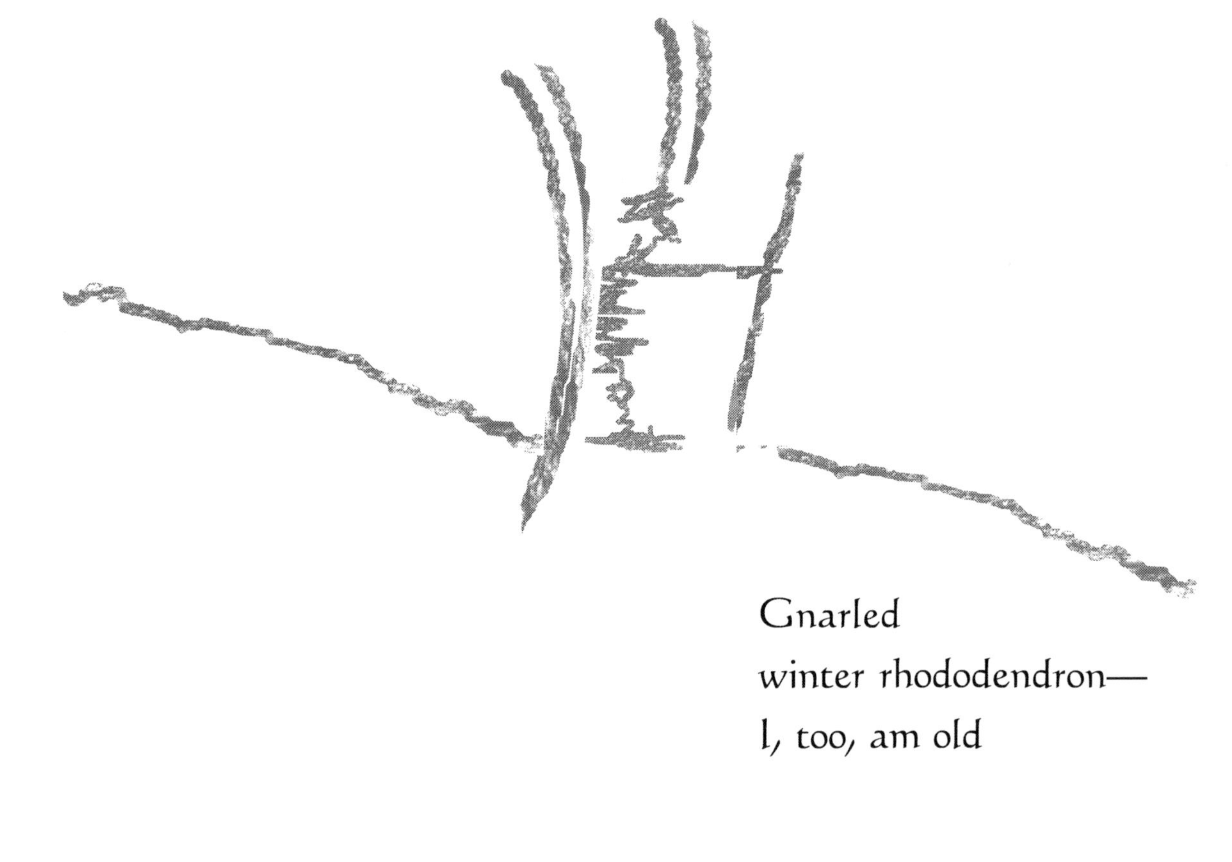

Gnarled
winter rhododendron—
I, too, am old

Douglas firs at dusk...
going home

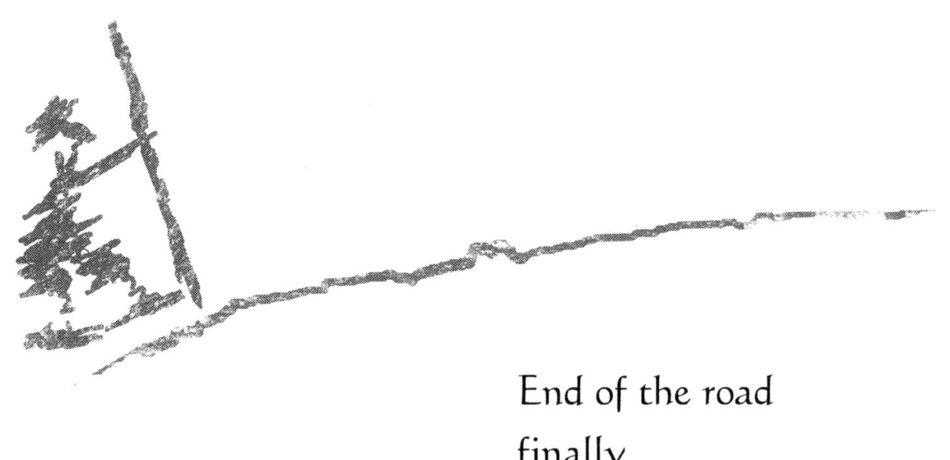

End of the road
finally...
Nature

Alone,
until you returned—
red butterfly

Blooming rose…
joy
in a flower

Dew in the rose…
my marriage

Why do we move?
so we can stand
still

Why do we stand still?

OK...

I'll sit down

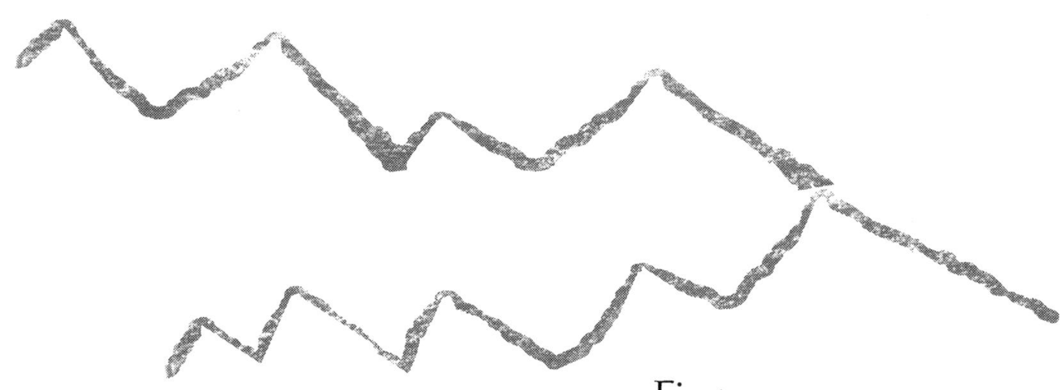

First snow...
scent of peppermint
winter's wind

At the river's edge…
waiting to cross over

Amongst the stones
no more
loneliness

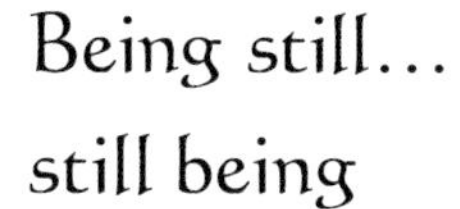

Being still…
still being

Clear and cold
in the night forest…
hoo, hoo, hoo

Here I am
here I stand
in Holy land

About the Author

Dr David H. Rosen is a physician, psychiatrist, and Jungian analyst. His interests include: finding meaning in suffering; dreams; spirituality as it relates to healing; and all kinds of creativity.

David is the author of twelve books, including *Transforming Depression: Healing the Soul through Creativity*; *The Tao of Jung: The Way of Integrity*; *Lost in the Long White Cloud: Finding My Way Home; Patient Centered Medicine: A Human Experience* with Uyen Hoang; *The Healing Spirit of Haiku* with Joel Weishaus; *Time, Love and Licorice: A Healing Coloring Storybook;* and *The Tao of Elvis* from Rosenberry Books. Dr Rosen is editor of the Texas A&M University Press twenty-volume *Fay Book Series in Analytical Psychology*. Rosen's books have been translated into many languages.

David was born in 1945 in Port Chester, New York, and attended University of California, Berkeley and the University of Missouri School of Medicine. He received psychiatric training at the University of California, San Francisco and subsequent training in Jungian analysis. He was the initial holder of the McMillan Professorship in Analytical Psychology at Texas A&M University (the first of its kind in the world), and is now Affiliate Professor in Psychiatry at Oregon Health & Science University.

Currently living in Eugene, Oregon, with his wife Lanara, David walks, paints and sees analytic patients. He also enjoys creating visual art, performing stand-up comedy, and writing haiku and ten-minute plays.

About the Artist

"If Salvador Dali's Don Quixote gave up tilting with windmills in favor of exploring the depths like a good Jungian … that is how I visulized the illustrations for *Spelunking Through Life*."

Diane Katz has illustrated many books of haiku, including *Learning to See the Truth; The Stone House; Beneath the Willow Tree*; and *In the Night Shallows*, which are available from Rosenberry Books.

Diane also created artwork for David Rosen's *The Tao of Elvis* and *Time, Love and Licorice: A Healing Coloring Storybook.*

She is currently illustrating *The Whistle Prayer* and is the author of *On All My Holy Mountain: A Modern Fraktur; Apples Dipped in Honey: A Jewish ABC;* and *The Story-Letters from Appletta Tooth Fairy.*

Through Rosenberry Books, Diane's work has been seen at the Metropolitan Museum of Art, the Smithsonian, the Chicago Institute of Art, Washington National Cathedral, etc. and is recognized by Design Observer of the Winterhouse Institute.

Diane lives with her husband in the woods of North Carolina.

Also of interest from Rosenberry Books and Wipf & Stock:

The Tao of Elvis by David H. Rosen, MD

"Magnificent … Truly a work of art. It brings to mind the inspired illuminated manuscripts of the Middle Ages." — Sue Monk Kidd, author of *The Secret Life of Bees*. In a most readable fashion, Rosen illuminates the inner Elvis and the myth of Elvis. Sumptuously designed and illlustrated.

Time, Love and Licorice:
A Healing Coloring Storybook
by David H. Rosen, MD

The attic is a wondrous place. It is a place to fix things: Dad's workshop is there, and Henry's special corner, which hides his secret supply of building blocks. When his soldier father comes back changed, Henry's fantastic block towers are threatened by Dad's sudden outbursts.

But in the attic inspirations come, and repairs of all kinds are made…

The drawings of Henry's optimistic, creative and imaginative world create a safe space in which children and families can face the disruptions of Post-Traumatic Stress Disorder (PTSD).